missing e.

Cut-up Poems from Tumblr

Simone Parker

Fernwood
PRESS

missing e.
Cut-up Poems from Tumblr
©2025 by Simone Parker

Fernwood Press
Newberg, Oregon
www.fernwoodpress.com

All rights reserved. No part may be reproduced
for any commercial purpose by any method without
permission in writing from the copyright holder.

Printed in the United States of America

Page design: Eric Muhr
Cover design: Nate Smith
Cover art: Efe Kurnaz on Unsplash

ISBN 978-1-59498-177-7

Dappled with lyrical Tumblr variations and prickly internet culture that have "held within the watery moon /of flash, forever online," Simone Parker's *missing e.: Cut Up Poems from Tumblr* explores how sexuality, identity, and love shape both (and vice versa). The reader, too, will share her longing for real connection in the twenty-first century: "i needed / to be kissed / my bitter naked thoughts." She delves deep into the chaos, knowing full well "trust is a sin on the internet. / Our galaxy a social experiment." Her scope seeks something larger than the human self, while not ignoring the power of desires within the interior, asking just how and why "[w]e are all yelling into bones and sand. Only a dead man offers eternity to the living." Playful and contemplative, Parker does offer hope, though with all the work, patience, and understanding it requires of us: "When universes are destroyed / and the sun is not a sun / will we still dance in the together."

—Rosebud Ben-Oni
Alice James Award winning author of
If This Is the Age We End Discovery

A page-turning tribute to the golden age of Tumblr—infused with fresh depth and emotional clarity. Insightful, uplifting, and full of life, these are simply great poems. The reader is transported into a three-dimensional world that feels both elevated and intimately familiar. This is a collection to keep under your pillow.

—Christian Wheeler
author of *Daydreams & Typewriter Smoke*

Traveling back in time, *missing e.* is a soothing balm for all of our formerly angsty teenage souls. Simone effortlessly captures the quirky nostalgia of Tumblr in a way that transports the reader back to simpler times.

—Abby Magalee
author of *Unstruck*

Simone Parker's *missing e.* activates a landscape where the "digital mundane" meets a girlhood both collective and singular. "I was a wild horse in your camera / roll; a moonmelon flower. Fruit / that grows (but not inherently) on an implausible Planet." Commingling the cut-up form popularized by Burroughs and revolutionized by feminist writers such as Dodie Bellamy with the collage-like and collaborative spirit of Tumblr, this collection achieves both a shimmering online polyvocality and a sharp autobiographical voice. Parker's centos glide us through a user's history of the platform: fandoms, nipple censorship, grave robbery, booping, 4chan, fake Scorsese films, etc., all the while forging new textures of queer self-writing. With the attention of an archivist, this aleatory poet and visual artist reblogs our own desires and affects: "all the things i wanted / to be (an angel, a ruse) / shifted inside me like / seasons of girlself." I emerged from this collection attuned to a kind of collecting that felt closer to expansive listening.

—Emily Skillings
author of *Fort Not* and *Tantrums in Air*

In *missing e.*, Parker explores the depths of Tumblr, a microcosm of the last fifteen years of the internet, as regulation, monetization, and censorship disrupt the grassroots tech optimism of the early 2010s and lead to the venture capitalist-funded cynicism of today, along the way making stops at highs and lows both personal and collective. This remarkable tapestry of a collection weaves a complex story of growing up online, intertwining niche discourse with global politics to expose in them the universal truths of ourselves and the homes we make on the internet. In its methods, observations, and style, *missing e.* is absolutely one-of-a-kind.

—Taylor Lorenz
author of national-bestseller *Extremely Online*

The living, breathing internet, endless in self-examination by a generation turned inward, suffers in certain regions from a dearth of sincerity. But if you hold it up to the light just right, plenty of places are doing just fine—and in the hands of poet Simone Parker, one of those places is Tumblr.

Parker's bold new collection of "cut-up poetry," *missing e.*, expertly repurposes the wild and proudly weird ecosystem of Tumblr to celebrate its contributors' stark confessions, plaintive ruminations, deliciously bizarre non sequiturs, and occasional polemic. A longtime devotee to (and student of) the Tumblr community and its myriad interior corridors, Parker assembles for our enrichment—and makes exceptionally pretty—a communitywide investigation of modern life. Assembled as they are in *missing e.*, no topic eludes Tumblr's wide eye and fearless exploration: consumerism, feminism, celebrity culture, current events of the 2010s and onward, body image, mainstream media's failings, nihilism, the madcap nature of our age, and (it can't be helped) Tumblr itself.

Invigorating and interpolating Tumblr's disparate narrative with intention and compassion, Parker's fresh compendium provokes thought, stirs emotion, plumbs Tumblr's extraordinary depth, and offers earnest homage to its soul and staggering variety. Parker, in her unforgettable collage, deftly usher's Tumblr's passionate clamor from the sparkling underbelly of the internet and into *missing e.*—a new and very special work of art.

—Zaq Baker
author of *Unspectacular*

for Ava

Contents

Acknowledgments 11
Introduction 13
I love you in the new year 15
The New England Vampire Panic 16
seventeen thousand dollars 18
Super and Who and Lock 20
girl autobiography 21
I Swear We Were Misha 23
A Creation Myth 24
missing e. 26
They Don't Say 28
[CENSORED] energy 29
an on and off switch 31
The Bone Discourse 32
I THINK I LOVE THE COLORS OF THE SKY UNTIL 34
There will be no sociology in the apocalypse 35
smoking sections 36

A Growing List of Banned Tags	37
Four Thirteen	39
Booped	40
still life of a romance	42
My body becomes a riot	43
The Morally Grey Cinematic Universe	45
Terms of Service	46
This is how it started, back then	47
Okay.	48
Gay Histories	50
No Courts at Pride	52
Confessional	55
The Military Skeletal Industrial Complex	56
4chumblr	58
Fake Story Mad Lib	59
Castiel's Girls	60
I Watch a Man Die on Television	61
Continues to Lose Her Entire Mind	62
it comes in twos	64
I've never watched an episode of Supernatural	65
The Cock Monologue	67
Pretty Girls	69
Snoem (Snail Poem)	70
Goncharov (1973)	71
Monster Girlfriend	73
THIS IS THE PLACE	74
Redemption	76
Tumblr Account as Doomed Narrative	78
Youth	80
Notes	81
Title Index	93
First Line Index	95

Acknowledgments

Thank you to the editors at *wildscape. literary journal*, where the poem "Confessional" was first published.

Thank you to Eric Muhr and Joann Boswell at Fernwood Press for all your work bringing this book to life.

Thank you to all the internet archivists at *Know Your Meme* and Tumblr blog *Meme Explainer* whose research has been invaluable to me in tracking down the origin and timelines of all the memes and internet events referenced in this collection.

Thanks to my friends Aaron Azar, Jaime Dear, Izzy Hall, and Ruben Otero, and YouTubers Sarah Z and The Digital Dream Club, for sharing your Homestuck knowledge.

To my family: Mom, Dad, Parker, Alex, and Ayelet. Thank you for your support. Thank you Karen Curry Parker for your expert counsel.

Thank you to my husband, Nate, for sitting through lengthy explanations of Tumblr lore, for representing the chronically offline perspective on these poems, for loving and bolstering me through bouts of self-doubt, and for being an amazing partner to me every day.

No words could be big enough to thank my best friend Ava, the reason I created a Tumblr account in the first place (damn you), my first and most passionate reader every time, my wisest sage and truest friend, the life of this and every party, the place where I feel most like me. Without you, none of this. Thank you.

Finally, thank you to everyone who had a hand in shaping Tumblr into the best, weirdest, cringiest hellsite corner of the internet. To the staff, current and former, and founder David Karp: thank you for your creation and stewardship of this space. If you ever get rid of the chronological dash and/or force infinite scroll on me I will revoke this thanks and possibly commit arson. Anyway, this thank-you is most of all for my fellow Tumblr users. You **are** Tumblr. Thank you to the gif makers, the shitposters, the artists, writers, lurkers, livebloggers, shippers, and fans. Thank you to all the creators who gave me the words for these poems. And thank you to my mutuals. It is a unique non-relationship we have, and one that I truly cherish.

Introduction

missing e. is a collection of cut-up poetry which endeavors to explore the history, politics, vernacular, and experience of Tumblr.com; to capture the complexities and eccentricities of a site which remains remarkably distinct from all other social media. Tumblr emphasizes anonymity over fame, community over individualism, chaos and financial ruin over monetization, and cryptids over influencers.

Unlike other social media sites, Tumblr uses a chronological dashboard, not an algorithm, to share posts with users, a feature which allowed me to travel back in time to previous years of my dashboard, from 2010–2024, to collect the text posts which would become the bones of this collection. To create these poems, I cut up and rearranged the words of my fellow Tumblr users, to tell the story of the day on which they were collected. Some are from specific days in international or Tumblr history—United States elections, Tumblr site policy changes, the first and only Tumblr fan convention—while others are less exceptional, representing the everyday Tumblr experience.

In the spirit of the-haiku-bot, this is a collection which finds poetry in the digital mundane while also speaking to the shared history of long-time Tumblr users, comprising events, controversies, and in-jokes that go many layers deep. We share a shorthand. Do not cite the deep magic to us—we were there when it was written. *missing e.* examines and celebrates that history, exploring the many facets of Tumblr: political discourse, queer experiences, fandom, the debate about leggings as pants (since settled but once extremely active on the pages of Tumblr.com), and much more.

Beyond the subject matter discussed on Tumblr, this collection is interested particularly in the way users speak, which is distinct from real life speech or the vernacular of other websites. In *missing e.*, Tumblr's unique verbiage is pulled apart and twisted back together into forty-four poems, illustrating shifts in language, tone, and topic on the platform over the fifteen years covered in this collection. In the interest of staying true to the Tumblr text style, some small "typos" have been left in.

In many ways, *missing e.* is a love letter to Tumblr or at least to my experience with it since I joined the site in January 2011. Tumblr is home to many varied communities and could never be wholly summed up in forty-four poems, but I hope with this collection to represent at least the sides which I have known these past fifteen years, and I hope some of them ring true to you, no matter whether you ever made a home on Tumblr.

P.S. I like your shoelaces.

I love you in the new year

January 1, 2014

sometimes, in secret,
we dissolved from the inside
within each other's perfect hands.
we'd bring stars, billions to
the gravestone of the moon, poor
thing, where little dewdrops form
on all your enemies, still fighting.

are you in love with me yet?
after the strength of holding blown out candles
in our eyes for a decade? when your skin is
falling, you still understand us, you yearn. think,

here is a person I could love!
our arms around the deep
upset animals of each other, our
brutal searing lips pressed together,
a raging smoke that wants you

always. like old fruit beneath
river flowers, aging intensifies pleasure.

The New England Vampire Panic

January 22, 2018

come forward;
a step further &

experience terrible things,
let it die

i, assassin
(anne rice catholic vampire angst,
the same shit),
giving a man extremism
like a gift on christmas.
he wants to unwrap
one (1) kind of violence.

media: he kills her while
playing deadpool and batman.
they are trying to imagine what
a second chance means.

confessing your love
in complete quietness?
the memory of how
we really do this every time?

each of us reads hate
messages and death threats
while turning on the tv for
the heathers remake hatewatch
(a microaggression inherently).
i can't ask for help
only social media attention
to reaffirm that everyone
will be mad, ya feel?

and where are my puritan vampires at?
still staring into space—
googled images of
ryan reynolds and ben affleck;
all we managed to agree on
is to love them.

seventeen thousand dollars

July 13–14, 2014
   DashCon, a fan-run convention for Tumblr users infamous for mismanagement, ends in a request for $17,000 in donations from attendees in addition to the paid ticket price. In exchange for donations, attendees are offered additional time in a tiny, inflatable ball pit.

For $17,000 USD
Tumblr users can purchase
a class action lawsuit;
my Night Vale ticket;
a meme about a ball pit disaster;
your dwelling place under that rock.

Still it remains
the con needs money asap.
pay with PayPal or
put it in the shitty deflated ball pit.
Allegedly money will be returned or
they'll get Benedict Cumberbatch.

I bought my ticket
buying into the con, then
time dragged on.
And we all waited.
Sitting in the panel room
at your shitty ass convention.

As I get more information
in the ball pit
the truth behind all this was
there is nothing.
No one will miss you,
DashCon disaster.

I was denied refunds for
the question:
Why is DashCon credit card fraud,
scamming a bunch of kids,
laughing at a joke

and bask in the memes.
Yes you can get
extra time in the ball pit
with the $17k.

Super and Who and Lock

October 13, 2013

I was a first born child 'til I gave
my soul up bleeding. I dipped a finger in
the time vortex—pale soft and transparent—
and was suddenly a ghost. A billion years
fell into the holy water and I could see it all:
the empire of nonexistence.

The first conscious years: humanity
a small boy nearing heaven only to fall
sacrifice; heart-angry brothers in a strange
universe; a locked church deep with song.

In the years of lonely ether
I hunted a wobbly dangerous light
like Gallifrey ablaze. Lucifer opens
his drunk eyes to watch the people burn.
Somewhere in that yawning flash
Sherlock Holmes sleeps naked.

Over smugly whispered deductions
I hold the time lords' screams
like stuffed animals at sleepovers.
I let the cat out at the gates of hell
and hear him say goodnight.

girl autobiography

April 1, 2019

he talks to me about
someone else's beauty.
i drink a cold brew
of jealousy and competition
and leave the phone on.

call me if you want to
get dinner or see me coming,
to fuck me while you say
things that Ruin My Life,
talking little miracles
into my ear (i don't
consider myself sexy;
he never said i was).

pray to him: stay,
i know i am not enough.
i need, i need.
april fools, i'd die for you.
you're an ass. i could
do your taxes for you.
im so mad. its on me.

i was taught from a young
age to help him,
to treat him well.
he will take it all away,
destroy me into someone else.

if i think i broke
the cycle of loving you,
i will neither confirm nor deny

but the presence of predators
at my funeral suggests
im the prey.

the person i am today
gazes off into the distance,
feral in an unfamiliar city—
wild animals don't have to be kind.

bold of you to assume i dont also
break my own dead body
before he can get to it.

I Swear We Were Misha

April 1, 2013
For April Fools' Day, the Supernatural *fandom executes an online flash mob event dubbed "The Mishapocalypse," changing all their profile pictures to photos of* Supernatural *actor Misha Collins and spamming their dashboards with photos of his face.*

The Mishapocalypse comes to you like
a Pit, a drug. Do you permit it?
Tumblr religion: we swear commitments
to untied shoes, badly written fanfics

and anti-possession symbols (I am
in total love with it). On this wrong
holiday we are all Misha. Perfection
is a cult on my dash, Misha's face

my diary. Misha Collins, help me
believe! I don't know whats real
anymore except that I'd happily kill
for you! We could rule the world,

tattooed and alive—poets to the overlord,
shamelessly taken by the angel sigil.
The power in that moment limitless,
sexual: a fandom in love with itself.

I don't regret the people we become
and forsake for a god or an angel
who hates himself. Our exposed secret:
we are going to die in search of Misha

and Misha will not remember us.

A Creation Myth

January 17, 2017

concept: woman making dear life,
peculiar new civilizations.
she takes water from the ocean,
dreams from her own subconscious,
and something personal, unconsciously,
as universal as nature or narrative—haunting.

and now that I Am,
find me in your life.
the gripping future plot
of our galaxy,
the ins and outs:

subconscious touching;
the moon that homecoming game
waiting, deeper in love;
ringing the doorbell.

i will be a sort of vodka aunt,
who teaches the child how to
kick moon rocks around
and what dreams mean.

if someone dies
don't look in its mouth,
instead make fucked up
terrifying deals with demons
to see each other again.

all the river riches disappear
into spruce forest smoke.
money screams from every direction,
her winnings, her symbolism;

does the woman act?
my wife, my witch,
how many violent planets
erupt in her theater?

and what, pray tell, do you take
from this slippery slope galaxy
now that it is destroyed?

missing e.

2014

Tumblr: a whole new species. Watch,
it becomes overridden with anxiety
and it's doomsday in your room.
Your useless content exceeds people
who wore leggings as pants:

I'm smarter / I read / I'm watching you /
I'm never leaving / they take us to worlds /
and you're left / pounding / teenage girls /
bumping into corners / stuck in the
vending machine / hissing at sunlight / I am
cruel / tired / I'm an adult.

I always stay indoors. I
show up and curse how uncool
I am: the scariest thing when mature
and (trying to be) self-sufficient.
My life is children's cartoons;
humor of humor; ice cream
out of the tub; a whole inside joke;
the club like if there's no food but
leggings. You're grounded.

Everyone tries to do things:
doesn't do things.

Two arms two legs
their mass and child, their firstborn.
A man, genuinely sorry for the people,
sometimes comments that
I am way too emotionally invested
in Teen Mom 2. If what I lack in
attractiveness is the thing, the light
from our laptops could tan us.

Personally, I used to want a fairytale:
Doctor Who, a Disney movie,
your favorite character. Imagine
how dark. A thousand miles away,
last night, morning. I feel like
Romeo, a bit sentimental,
like when I created my list
of all the reasons why to hate
is like your name. Now I have
absolutely no idea how to get off.

You look so pretty, yes,
and I didn't realize
all the times we've dreamed
that we regularly go to sleep
before 10 p.m. It's confusing
but I'm pretty sure by now
it's just part of the City
and I kinda get it a little bit.
Now I am a person
that wears my personality
description as pants.

They Don't Say

July 29, 2014

on tumblr they don't say "i love you" they say

"compassion extends from me
arm to arm, flows in pure tides
flowering in organs, in telomeres
a heaven brutally executed like
a sun at night too pretty to erode.
I want to wash this sleepy life
in human nature, to shave my
armor away, soft and bloody, for
you to brighten my aging rooms
and disturb my dark with sour
sensibilities. there is so much
good in the family u make."

and i think that's beautiful.

[CENSORED] energy

December 3, 2018
Often called the Great Purge of 2018. Following the removal of the Tumblr app from Apple's App Store due to a reported issue with pornography and CSA materials, Tumblr announces a ban on all adult content sitewide.

"your nipples are now
a sin zone"—our anti-horny initiatives
whispered this into my ear.
can't cum until @staff decide
you're allowed to.
the cybernetic code
to shame mankind,
ban female-presenting nipples
(our collective nipples),
and welcome
actual pedophiles.

i've got some nipples to present
to god herself, st. agatha, and tumblr staff,
watching the chaos they created
with their own reflection—
the newest tumblr purge:
ban everything horny
(also we're not banning
the nazis still).

ancients of tumblr: follow me.
i offer you a titty or just
the nipple, a space for softness.
i would hate for each titty
to fall into nihilism
in this nipple discourse.
it would be blasphemous.

staff logging in as you delete
your blog for my nipples,
whether they're "female
presenting" or "god presenting."
I Still Follow.

i will, of course, remain.
for my own sanity i still
wouldn't move to twitter.
i'd prefer to whisper
my post to the worms.

an on and off switch

March 7, 2021

My gender is a
little cat on a windowsill,
like bread at the last supper,
this continued gulf
between our selves, younger and older.
I just woke up a year ago.

Oh to be
a comic relief character,
a Jewish comedian
so loud that you
don't seem to understand that
something is wrong.

What a time to be alive
as hope rots on the vine
of the internet
and you died in silence
after years of viewing it.

The Bone Discourse

December 17, 2015
  Tumblr user fuckinheathen is accused of stealing human bones from cemeteries for witchcraft in a scandal sometimes called #boneghazi.

I dream of a black dog, a Grim
standing guard over the altar
of Tumblr dot com, righteous.

Today's offering: Tumblr user
fuckinheathen and all the dead
ever buried, corpses turning in

the Bone Discourse (children, friendly
reminder to ethically source your anxieties
about Death). When I die, tie my bones deep

so that they stay buried. When you die,
collectors paint white flowers on
your skull. They long for your teeth

on the altar, your bones the epicenter
of their need. In dark college parties,
I watched their necromancy overwhelm,

knee-deep in coffins for black magic
rites in front of the burning students,
eating outrage and degradation like salt.

It became tradition, those four years,
digging backyard graves at the frat;
making desecrated dirt offerings before

occult leaders; handmaidens bringing
heart-selling hexes and remains of hospital
priests, stolen, bodies drained to place

on bone collectors' altar beds. Good ol'
necromancers, practicing dishonor
over loved ones' remains, burying the price

and digging it up over and over, never satisfied,
never laid to rest. Magic is a bloody shovel
with Death cast in its guts. Who were they?

The actual human people, ancestors of
ancestors, they steal from the dirt?
Who is faint on salty knees for them?

Survivors before the Grim, the broken
crypt—whose family was stolen to offer
Black bodies to a curse? To a meme?

The Louisiana rains wash up racist
text messages and little bits of bone—
witnesses, out of heaven—bowls of honey

and acrylic paint, secret prayers swept
into the street. The police dogs tear
into mundane memory. The dead are gone.

What remains but veneration? What
remains but empty coffins and pissed-off spirits,
dogs and their bones? New Orleans parties

and rises, nothing immortalized save for a
deeper burial. We are all yelling into bones and sand.
Only a dead man offers eternity to the living.

I THINK I LOVE THE COLORS OF THE SKY UNTIL

March 9, 2013

I CONFESS to Jane, a lesbian:
my secondhand religion
is breaking apart in the ends
of her hair, cut short or ripped
off, so husky it could break me.

Slip it off, she says, like embarrassment,
to the east. To the sky, about to turn
precious with sun. Be water, spilling
into my wants without fear.

Jane gets head. We press palms
and pleasures, glistening.
It's a kind of voyeurism
to watch her harsh passions
writhe in the light of a mirror,
a reciprocal joy to learn her
blazing pink tapestry.

My own hand is new on her chest.
The sky, our witness, colors
into dawn, yellow and rapturously warm.
I'm so in love with her morning mouth,
vulnerability alight in day bloom,
the color of the sky quietly singing
the universe we are while she sleeps.

There will be no sociology in the apocalypse

November 17–18, 2012
    Former Disney Channel actor and prominent Tumblr user Cole Sprouse deletes his Tumblr, explaining the entire account was a "social experiment."

This is how it happens—
you worship the wrong guy.
Take a moment to remember
dreams about a traveling son
transformed into one of you;
some experimental thing
like a resurrected Savior.

Followers, let us all join
hands and reconsider
this friendship.
Cole is gone,
a lesson for us.

We stand betrayed,
wronged by Him
who joined this website
and let us believe.

Trust is a sin on the internet.
Our galaxy a social experiment.
Cole says good night, the end
of days is near. A white girl
breaks her iPhone and
I follow.

smoking sections

May 25, 2016

i was out of smokes
in a failed forest
writing a fiction of you

our relationship
a lost cigarette
with same-gender guilt

you were french
in the story
combating modern illnesses

i asked who will love
the obsolete things
you live with

you allowed no curiosity
my petty lips bled
snow came in rust-ignorant drops

real you was
outside smoking
powerful uncaring

i needed
to be kissed
my bitter naked thoughts

two mothers said i'm
hard to love
i nodded understanding

jealous of your unaware
guilty thinking
you could spare me one

A Growing List of Banned Tags

December 25–26, 2021
Apple's new app store content guidelines trigger Tumblr to briefly institute a site-wide ban of posts tagged with a number of common search terms, including #girl.

December took with it like sex searches.
Tumblr banned creators content full-scale
(the infamous Great Purge of 2018,
banning all female-presenting nipples,
wasn't good enough), but tags newly
means money for Apple.

Due to Apple's content rules
(who kiss gayly),
censorship is strict.
dark TikTok, Apple war, iOS trust filtering,
girlban: censorship MCU.
Blogs in Purge on their follower's dashboards.
THE BIG ONE: "protecting the children."

"Because of potentially suggestive or explicit content"
g*rls is banned but
here's the real kicker:
there aren't men kissing,
tags such as #mine, #my stuff,
triggers and content warnings,
shit like cottagecore and 500 Muppets.
your fictional universe, flagged as explicit.

Kids on TikTok saying "k1ll" and "d34d,"
go complain about the war on #girl to Apple.
Marvel up at the war dashboards,
infamous community vs. new draconian tactics.
as the incidental children of the blog changes,
you who protest their romantically knowing organization:
comply less.

Gatekeep this godforsaken platform.
Fuck an in-app transaction.
Have gay sex in Apple's walled-garden.

I complete their fuck-you message:
"This content has been hidden."
That's weird. Anyways.

Four Thirteen

October 25, 2011
  *Homestuck Act 5 finale "[S] Cascade" is released, leading
  fans to crash host sites Newgrounds, MS Paint Adventures,
  and Megaupload.*

When universes are destroyed
and the sun is not a sun
will we still dance in the together?
Still dream running naked
in the streets of our fandom?

Soon flowers explode from the beautiful
irony of websites destroyed.
Soon we'll realize a new suffering
in the two in the morning somewhere,
the world we've seen still to come,
a puddle of light awaiting her seer.

On a meteor-beaten planet an exile
places her hand on my bifurcated heart,
the tornado stilling, tumorless.

On Earth a kid stands in his bedroom
dying. That windy thing of a universe
crying out for him to ascend.

My good dog, my best friend
a god, wringing radioactive rings to ash.
Destruction making us love the immense
forms of our friends, listening to words
from their rose lips so magnificent I could cry.

These squealing years on Newgrounds
we'll be able to look back on, powerful
and green, held within the watery moon
of flash, forever online.

Booped

> *April 1, 2024*
>   *For April Fools' Day, Tumblr introduces a feature allowing users to "boop" one other with an image of a cartoon cat paw.*

a cat paw
the closeness i want: this
wretched thing, real
human whimsicality.
i yearn.

keep booping me beloved
but make it hurt.
kiss with tongue or cum
i don't care. i was once

prolific. i loved things deeply and
straight from the heart
but today i just scrolled
in front of you with
any machine, waiting

to be booped passionately.
our joke love
language; inspired button
embodiment of want;
a solution to being
in this apocalyptic wasteland.

the paws appear;
blood sweat and tears.
better kill me in one shot.
better make it count babe.
smack your phone trick paw
upon my clit, pure and honest
like a bear. i'm a tumblr user
about to be born. wake

up, ceaseless booper, i
have so much to become
if you'll let me.

still life of a romance

September 12, 2015

talent is overrated but when you said
paint is your second language

i fell in love. blueberries loose
in your apron, sunset strewn

across my body, my feminine heart
a halved strawberry on a cake.

were u tempted? for all your dexterous
talking about want, didn't you still

flirt clumsily with my open flames?
eyelids burning and blinking bad poems,

a wine-softened romance. feelings ran
slowly from the bottle over our clothes,

our legs. i wanted to track the deep truths
of your laughter as it sang off key

in my ears. in the morning when
the paint breaks down, i'll keep

every plastic flake next to my car keys
like a victory. my own wicked hoarding

in praise of you. you, erupting into
some intense, unfortunate thing like me.

My body becomes a riot

June 24, 2022
  The United States Supreme Court overturns Roe v. Wade.

girl i'm sorry i think
it's not girl summer for the
Supreme Court.

my whole body becomes
a riot. a miscarriage
of the law.

welcome to America, everyone
(baby i'm not even here)
where i'm fantasizing about being alive,
about pleasure, healthcare
that's not dangerous,
and the towering privacy of abortion
in a state that outlaws it.

i started focusing on what it's like
doing the right thing.
activist girl summer
fighting anti-abortion authorities
with Facebook discourse posts.
potential energy pushing back.

the American people are
seeking an abortion, trying to remove
legislation from a uterus, a federal right:
you should know better!

part of yourself moves on
and forgets (so you can feel
good) that your health data
can be used against you.

politicians can sell state of mind, your health
within their jurisdiction,
they, my abusers, have forgotten it's
their own fault.

idk i just personally am fantasizing
about a conservative majority
that can be killed.

The Morally Grey Cinematic Universe

October 8, 2019

I wish I loved him in the 19th century,
a hothouse flower between his hands.
He loves me like a woman not a person,
going apeshit all the time, jealousy heavy

in his tired liver. On the sidewalk outside
7/11, I wait to be plucked. My
extremist, my moral grey. I'm
the woman of his universe, inferior.

He can diagnose me, a hint of Sharpie
marker and a knife he pulled out, the
middle still cold. His hard liquor passion,
crying, kisses my intestines, my kidneys,

a type of personal terrorism. I turn them
out onto the table to waste and become
no less than psychotic, an incoherent thing
trying to remake me different, braver, happy.

My new organs—savage, whole—will
taste sweet like nuance and religious wine.
I'll live off compliments from other girls
and hate and hate and hate.

Terms of Service

March 24, 2012

The rules of the game change
and I match them, keeping safe
standing there with Michelle—still waiting—
and also with you
pushing daisies in my hand

like a little baby.
I see it all so clearly in my head
it's killing me:

the doctors working;
gun
ever in his favor;
and the person you most need.
Cabin pressure pushing everyone
to the death.
Blink and I fear I miss it.

The forecast today says
we'll survive—today
is not that day; both get to live.

But when she does, when she kills him
you just hear the fireflies
crying "not everyone gets out alive.
We do not condone."

Well it may be a blessing love dies
instantly—like muffled background noise—
without reading the atmosphere.

This is how it started, back then

July 20, 2022

we burst into giggles—
to open the bottle
in people's basements,
down a rabbit hole.

some flowers and a cake, post-hyperpop
her lesbian friends who had
consenting sexual partners!
how ridiculous!—
i was going to make her a Cult

of Dionysus.
i want to live life.
i'm sick of being poor:
emergency funds
the stuff of our lives,

music scenes in the internet era.
indie musicians and laptop musicians
waste knowledge and time and energy on causes
deliberately to offend god.

his dead friends
talk to the electronic music
(everybody shut up and I'm fine)
if you want to hear,
i've been keeping a list of
every used drug in existence—
also cake—
read them in your study bible.
read them in your guinea pig instagram accounts.

i just want to have some enjoyment for once
so we're not caught unawares.

Okay.

November 8–9, 2016
    Donald Trump is elected President of the United States for the first time.

It's in our history
(shriveled, bigoted):
Life, liberty, and the pursuit
of checks and balances.
A fucking rampage
in our nation's highest office,
in our genetic makeup.

                Is it okay?

How deep your open sore
colonial ancestors are
in the garbage pit of this country?
Somewhere a clock is ticking.
Somewhere bigotry exhales.

                It's not okay

tonight. It's all bad. This morning
is not happening. When will
Donald Trump die? Better,
get assassinated? A president
has been assassinated

                okay.

Congress going to church
for a sexual assault trial
adjusted for modern values.
We're humiliated so much
after our own catastrophe,

validated but through quiet,
dishonest red tape, that life hell
his government

        okays.

Wriggling anger fills up your dashboard,
no take backs. Fired parents send thoughts
to the guns that took their children,
to the violence we'll die because
and there will be heads down, IGNORING,
frictionless, and you'll vote

        like it's okay.

You'll look out for one another,
and VOTE and VOTE and VOTE.

        It's okay—

I'm here. You're motherfucking here
(in Hell-region, threatened).
Even if all you can do is
Loving your children furious,
the people we owe it to.

        Okay but

don't fail me. Even a downhill spiral
will be stripped from us,
contested, like all political
children's lives, like all reason
and rightness, grieved but not

        okay.

Gay Histories

July 20, 2022

i stood next to him
in the homes of lesbians,
a sense of sheer terror,
completely, totally believing:
something (my high school gsa?
depictions of gay and bi people
in media?) was accelerating
the end of the world.

my father's dead friends.
refuse to handle the bodies.

we deigned to care—
writing down their memoirs.
as he tried not to cry over
the knowledge of this pain—
to lay these people to rest
with little intervention.

the few straight allies pitched in
and saw their pale, pained faces
going out of their way to find
all the lgbt books to read or reread.

it's not information that people have
nowadays. i was six years old but
i remember when
i remember
and i relived it
taken great pains to write it down
easing suffering
but i feel the pain of every single person leaving

(just a little younger than me)
less deserving of dignity and life,
on the front page!
as they died by the thousands.

No Courts at Pride

June 26, 2015
*   The United States Supreme Court grants marriage equality in all fifty states.*

today is monumental.
I wake up with new rights and
you can hear the mic drop from
the Supreme Court

                                    still, do you feel safe?

this morning I spend my entire heart
for Ruth Bader Ginsburg,
shout proud romantic screams for her,
for my newly voiced love.

                                    straight people patting
                                    themselves on the back.

done counting nights from Stonewall to today:
history made, a beautiful universe, and I am here
celebrating, magically, across 50 states at once.

                                    the bare minimum is
                                    not evidence of kindness.

tonight, America is my girlfriend.
she's down on her knees
to offer legal protection & benefits
like a ring

                          a lapse in cruelty by the supreme court.
                                    marriage equality,
                                  for homosexuals only. but
                        to the folks for whom this decision
                          doesn't address the injustices?

a party in federal hall, legal marriage & gay sex.
maybe the Westboro Baptist Church is on fire,
making chemical music while I dance.

                              the struggle is FAR from over.
homeless lgbtqa youth, trans and gender non-conforming persons:
                              we will not forget you.

even if the negativity is always there,

                              we will not ignore you.

the future looks pretty bright.

                              we will not silence you.

I will not suppress my celebration screams!

                              celebrate if you want to,
                            if you've forgotten all the bad.
                                    fuck I'm trying
                                but I know the cost

PROGRESS IS GOOD.

                            decades of fighting and
                            we still face discrimination,
                              violence, homelessness.
                              there will be backlash.
                my hunger pains will not let me sleep.

GOD we are allowed to be happy

                    our community who committed suicide,
                                and who will:
                                    I know you,
                        fighting to keep your eyes open.

ONE DAY OF HAPPINESS

I'm sorry.
you deserved real equality,
a lifeline.

BE ANGRY TOMORROW.

I imagine them all growing up,
maybe to fall in love, or
a thousand other whispered things—
so happy.

I am so happy.

me, I am collapsing
onto the rainbow flag
and with my last ounce of strength,
I do believe,
without evidence, in freedom.

Confessional

April 1, 2013

when i was little i
pretended to be a statue
of an astronaut, but not
the astronaut himself.

all the things i wanted
to be (an angel, a ruse)
shifted inside me like
seasons of girlself.

the secret changes
my best friend and i felt
together, the supernatural
want i held in my diary.

how confusing it is
to want to be loved
knowing girls don't
fall in love with girls.

The Military Skeletal Industrial Complex

October 2014
    A tweet by Twitter user dril referencing "the skeleton war" picks up steam on Tumblr, kicking off a long-running meme about a fictional "Skeleton War" in which skeletons battle with an enemy army of "fuckboys."

Do you have a skeleton?
I think I saw him
trapped in a stolen internet
or somewhere in the ditch.
Outta grave they forget
all children claimed
by the Skeleton War.

Hope-kissed bones
to your children, good
skeleton soldier farewells.
It felt wrong to be cool
in my comfort coffins
surfing the web as
bloody insides lay
exchanged at my kitchen
table, fallen into draft.

Where are the skeletons
you lived for? Stripped of
skin, yet to be found.
Darling, every fibula of you
is a shed tear in my selfish hand,
distracted dreaming waxing
dead at your funeral.

I would put my phone down
to return home. To be girls
decoding text messages
on Halloween, skeletons still
in exalted teen peace (as if
that ever existed) found
when they die, stuck
and emotional, six feet under
the fuckboys but still
none the weaker.

4chumblr

November 14–15, 2010
   Posts on notorious forum site 4chan announce a planned (ultimately unsuccessful) hack on Tumblr.

it's a vulgar rain and the water asking
what is the source of this war?

a threat: they will find the
private places we go to die

set fire to the tea party we're playing
shipping club turned gore roulette

panic eating conspiracy or
kitten photo rebuttals to survive

a black hole 4chan invasion
glorified into naïve anticlimax

less typhoon than goldfish
the porn unhidden the violence

low and pretty its dark face
imaginary like errors on the moon

the anonymous universe come to
die or to fuck (a raging proposal)

websites anthropomorphized
into cute new beings, deviant proxies

a phenomenon: we draw them in love
hacked but with sex we ship this so hard

4chan users enjoy
your tumblr account

Fake Story Mad Lib

2013–2019
Made up of World Heritage Posts from throughout the years. These are famous, impactful, and historical Tumblr posts. The name is a play on UNESCO World Heritage Sites.

OH MY GOD the _____ thing happened today.
　　　　　　　　SUPERLATIVE

My _____ and I went to the _____ and
　　AUTHORITY FIGURE　　　　　　　AMERICAN-CODED EVENT

there was this homeless _____ there with
　　　　　　　　　　　　OCCUPATION

a _____ sign. I _____ over and handed him
　POLITICAL SLOGAN　　VERB (PAST TENSE)

_____ dollars. Suddenly he took off a _____,
　NUMBER　　　　　　　　　　　　　　　　　ARTICLE OF CLOTHING

revealing he was actually _____! "You are the best,
　　　　　　　　　　　　MALE CELEBRITY

most _____ person in the world," he cried,
　　　ADJECTIVE

and _____ me in front of all the _____ He
　　VERB (PAST TENSE)　　　　　　　　　PLURAL NOUN

started _____ and singing "_____ Homeless
　　　VERB ENDING IN ING　　　　　　EXCLAMATION

Style!" Out of nowhere a _____ full of _____
　　　　　　　　　　　　VEHICLE　　　　　　NATIONALITY

people in "Down with _____" shirts screeched up and
　　　　　　　　　PRIVILEGED IDENTITY

started _____ me. I yelled, "Hewp me pwease,
　　　VERB ENDING IN ING

Mr. _____!" He walked over and gave one of them
　　SAME MALE CELEBRITY

a _____. "It's all going to be _____," he told
　DISPLAY OF AFFECTION　　　　　　　　ADJECTIVE

them and they began to cry. The crowd bellowed,

"I _____ IT!" And everyone _____.
　　WATERCRAFT　　　　　　　CELEBRATORY VERB (PAST TENSE)

Castiel's Girls

September 21, 2013

the gay angel breaks
your lollipop heart in half and spits
it out into your coat collar.

you look cool like that, licking
songs off the hand of his bad moods.
bravest men in love with all those
sensitive death strings, and how
well he gives blowjobs in haunted
ramen restaurants. the people

you have a crush on still scream
wishing-machine stereotypes over him,
their prayers of profanity getting
more addictive, smoking the smooth
heat of the falling moment.

they hate the female character—who
gets no name—for her blond,
for her female, for her spit on
his hand. you bit that

lollipop girl and spit and
spit. pull your houses like
noodles out of hell just
to break down, supernatural
emotions drinking you into bed.

after. after. i am become
the female character i hate.

I Watch a Man Die on Television

January 15–16, 2012

We all saw the picture: victim on a hot
sauce landscape. A world soured and rich,

sick with alcoholic calmness,
watching a murder out the window.

The streetlights come on queasy now,
as if to resurrect his wrists, still falling

through the snow of 64 missed calls,
each one cutting different emotions

from his body. A vicious nighttime sky
makes witnesses of the insomniacs

at Walmart. They pick up razors, Nutella.
They think about suffering, grace.

We all saw the night destroying our dead.
We all moved together, away.

Continues to Lose Her Entire Mind

February 23, 2023

spiritual wellness culture:
luxuries that white women are

falling in love with / whole heartedly prefer / consider
    "necessities"
(there's absolutely nothing wrong with that)

a clarity of purpose ripped from us
for assholes like elonjeff muskbezos
to replace with a new book or
kickass female leads,
such a good song and chocolate
hazelnut ice cream—

making us miserable on purpose!
go inside and touch
your phone lock screen,
your internet rabbit hole
for support.

women want so badly.

to be girly
to be deemed (un)worthy of male attention
so fucking badly

having our femininity
wrestled and failed

to make me take joy in
shaking and shivering
in the freezer with a homemade
breakfast burrito. it's chilly but
what are "luxuries" to the spirit?

nice things and indulgences?
eating fat little babies with gruel
proved very delicious.

good food and 50–150k followers
doesn't make me a damn hypocrite—
like yes bitch I'm wealthy, but

I'm spending today thinking
I will never accomplish anything in life.

it comes in twos

April 23–24, 2015

at 2 in the morning
dreamy girl sighs dissipate
from a bitter cigarette
shortened and so cold.
i just couldn't let you sleep.

on the roof outside your window
(i remember this scene)
the stars that are sometimes cameras
picture me as dust, clairvoyant.

here's the time bomb:
how pretty we'll fall.
when i say it out loud
you reply with sarcastic
cynicism: oh my god
You Cannot Rest Here.

ah but when i slip out of control
the miserable paradox of things
you say are unforgivable,
start to unravel
a swarm electric.

it's better to kill the idea—
wisdom, murder it—
and better to rot.

I've never watched an episode of Supernatural

November 5-6, 2020
   The election of Joe Biden coincides with the canonization of popular ship Destiel *from* Supernatural.

Get your bottles ready,
jaw clenched over a Zoom call: 2020
drops another bomb on us.
Make Jensen Ackles start
an apocalypse, an election.

Like whats worse?
That angel dying of homophobia
or the official Oreo's brand account
doing batshit stuff
to reach a modern audience
(in an internet brainrot kinda way)?

The mood in here is electric
I just woke up bleeding
from the eyes, Covid's still climbing
and god it's not funny!
Destiel's real—yes!
Destiel isn't actually canon—

Fuck this is what I mean!
It's time-traveling collective catharsis,
like a Cole Sprouse social experiment.

If people could see
god is choosing these events;
writers choose the plot
the single most buckwild night,
and all you can think about is
what? Georgia, Pennsylvania, Nevada?

They killed Cas
for Vladimir Putin
for TikTok
for my Ao3 history.

The Cock Monologue

May 2015
An unknown Tumblr user edits a post by author John Green about reaching 200,000 followers on Tumblr to instead be about the ecstasy of performing fellatio. The subsequent fallout of this post leads Green to leave the site, and Tumblr to remove the feature allowing users to edit one another's posts.

My candy mouth, drained
of your salt, wants you
back, wants you crazy.*

I'm running far
on my heels, running
down your throat—
a cause I cannot follow
cannot be satisfied.

All my slobbering honesty
tastes hot, a hairball
down my throat. I cannot
speak to you with that

smell on me, powerful
and sticky like craze,
like cum. You look
at me. Near, nearer.

At your favorite dock
a boat proceeds.
I ask the salted fish
when is it enough?

I can be intense
isn't it good?
You say no.
You say no.

I wipe your energy
off on my arm.
I wipe your slobber
off on my neck.

All that honest feeling
pumped out only to say
I'm over.

*Disclaimer: The word "crazy" is used in this poem for the sake of maintaining the integrity of "The Cock Monologue" as it appeared on Tumblr in 2015. This word, which traces back to the Middle English word "crasen" meaning to be crushed, cracked, diseased, or deformed, is inextricably linked with discrimination, oppression, and mistreatment of people with mental illness. Simone Parker and Fernwood Press denounce use of this word generally and stand with advocates for mental health in their fight for better understanding, resources, and protections for people with mental illness.

Pretty Girls

March 30, 2020

every girl i see is pretty,
so mediocre
so beautiful next to me

i met a girl, so was struck by lightning
in the best possible way.
i felt my soul, and touched it
briefly. i made a pretty girl laugh
more than the rest ever will.

this pretty girl.
oh i just wanted
for a solid 10 minutes
to turn the music down,
put her hands on my hips,
give her my coffee order,

to art, to laugh;
years happen at the same time.

i asked her where she was heading
and she said "the pandemic is over."
i cried right in front of her.
she was so painfully pretty,
even to a woman made from clay

with a knife and fork.
humans were made pure,
no thoughts, empty word doc
and a blue checkmark:
failure. legend.

you don't know what to do with yourself. me,
im trying to restart my daydream.

Snoem (Snail Poem)

April 23–24, 2015

You cannot sleep now
the sunshine says
outside the stained windows
of snurch (snail church).

When a spooky child grows up
what is she but a woman?
A snake (snail snake)
or golden crowning swarm?

Let her be quiet and placid,
pretty but always with some
unforgivable flaw. You'll see.
Instant prejudices forge snonsters

(snail monsters) and the girls
dedicated to recovery, sick
with clairvoyant naivety
playing white noise and

calming rainforest sounds.
Don't you remember? That dark
little snace (snail space), the air
all sighs? Crumbs and giggles

at our lips like bees? In my head
I was there for snenturies (snail
centuries). In my head I am
there now. The girls are shrieking

picking snowers (snail flowers)
for bitter friends in miserable
affection. Everything that changes you
controlled in joy parentheses.

Goncharov (1973)

November 23, 2022
    Tumblr users collaboratively invent a fake Martin Scorsese mafia film titled Goncharov.

Goncharov is a dream.
it's the ability to see those ancient stories,
like a half-remembered invention.
fake film written in fake memory
transported through fractal fiction images.

you all are casting shadows you
cannot nail down. isn't it beautiful?
perfect reflection of a thousand other films.

motifs of homoerotic tension,
Cold War propaganda, of fate and tragedy:
subversion of a public
disinformation campaign, but
not a loveless one.
there is no right or wrong in a dream.

at the end of the movie which is
not a movie
Katya points a gun:
our fictions are running
out of time before death.

if we stop it is unclear
what happens to them.
when the meme dies down
what else dies with it?

i wonder how it will be remembered.
lovingly, the head of the family

bleeds inevitably into
the natural cycle
of forgotten memetic trends.

Monster Girlfriend

July 29, 2014

i will be a timeless astronaut
if you'll be my demon girlfriend

our first date to a star
our 2nd to billions of other universes

when you're grumpy on birthdays
i will smooch you happy

remember time is only that which
slows the process of healing

life is only afterlife and, like you,
is much too pretty at night

there's no repair in a vampire love
no heaven in endless intermission

but no magic in the pure white
world you don't darken

i would give up all my human to
erode, sunless and unaging, with you

THIS IS THE PLACE

> *May 20, 2013*
> *Yahoo announces their purchase of Tumblr for $1.1 billion.*
> *Six years later, it will be valued at only $3 million.*

dear yahoo,
the person i
reblogged this from
deserves to be happy.

a teenage girl says
there will be a war,
the romantic kind,
on our dash.

we laugh at the judge.
we know there is
nothing here worth
1.1 billion.

yahoo, or
john f kennedy,
remove the post limit
that is all we ask for.
scroll through the weight
of full human emotions:

here comes the smut
with all the boys,
not an angel to tumblr's
exact standards;
the wonder you threw

across the room,
so red. like freaking out
or GUILTY for doing
nothing wrong !!

she wears a lot of feels.
she knows—crying,
hugging him tight,
comforting to kill himself—
if he sought the lord
you are bastardizing them.

you just sit there.
tumblr was bought out. shit.
i'm not 15 anymore.
nor you.

yahoo bought tumblr.
tumblr users like you
made them watch it burn,
for $1.1B.

Redemption

July 31, 2024
DashCon 2 is announced.

Is it too late to be a deep
and profound object?
Am I forever a strange
invention of Tumblr,
ruined by unfathomable
temptations (10,000 pics
of women and your
slutty slutty rats)?

Consider that historical
ball pit, that geode.
an ancient convention
inside, a messy piece
of art. do you remember?

DashCon—a kind of
biblical tragedy still
quivering in the pit
of my worm self,
destined to destroy.
Accepted into canon
as a masterpiece lost
in sparkling orbit.

Now, with my life
and the economy
in sharp shambles
it reveals a second life.

Faith (meaning: a world
where Destiel is canon)
crash into me.
Into millions of
Tumblr users.
Every ruined place
unended, back from
2014. For us.

Crack open the
worst con to see
what is perfect.
Taste the burnt
income, fulfilling.
It reflects a better
world: a ball pit
saved, justified.

I vow to love
what is messy,
to spend my
humanity with
you weird freaks
in Toronto.

Tumblr Account as Doomed Narrative

2013–2019
World Heritage Posts

I was a wild horse in your camera
roll; a moonmelon flower. Fruit
that grows (but not inherently)
on an implausible Planet,
a fertile Heaven and Purgatory.

You were a gentle schoolgirl
feeding it to DashCon attendees.
Human teeth and utopian ideals
lapping red-faced out of your palm.

This is a study of the unreliable
narrator. [the skeletons ooh]

You found me by statistical error,
by escalation of disbelief. We were
telling propaganda in the school bus
screeches, misled imagination buzzing
at the window. I tasted then that sweet
fruit, invisible but for a willingness

to believe. We sat like sirens in the blue
distance while you carved colonies
into my arm, revealing the milky flowers
of our bones. Spiders and sweet tea sank
to my lips, a vibrant poison but one I
was panting for. Such ardent desperation
for cheap pleasure. The first seeds
of doubt too much to swallow.

I knew before you tapped on the window.
I knew before you cut my urgent hand.
All the after already embroidered in our
shoelaces, brutal and exaggerated. Still I
drank it cold, like water reclaimed
from that sour cave under your dress.

The narrator stretches her authority.
When a woman does magic there is no
recovery, only a swarm of manipulated
daughters, empty caskets on the water
drifting gentle like parsley. All that's salty
tastes bitter, all generosity dwindling to
almosts. Then perish.

Youth

September 2011

A beautiful moment:
I can hear your
footsteps, a goodbye

and now we are left pretending
to enjoy the company of this
awkward, embarrassing world.

All I want is magic.
Every day I wake up
and do not go to Hogwarts
the excitement plummets.

I want to believe in my feelings.
I want to believe in
anything Please!

I can forgive you if
for me, you'd please pretend
these blog posts are more than just
subtle signals for want,
touching you boldly with
a hand you'd never feel, sobbing
COME LOVE ME. I
WILL NEVER UNDERSTAND YOU.

In a couple years I will look back at my Tumblr
all this young vulnerability and pretty time-wasting,
my little heart spilled across a blank page
(how quickly time has flown by).
It turns out that I was always
so strong.

Notes

The text posts cut up to create this work appeared on the poet's Tumblr dashboard on the listed date, but in some cases were written prior to that date. Text posts cut up to create the poems in this collection were written by the following Tumblr users:

"I love you in the new year"
>thinkingstaring, weltenwellen, snime, 2treehill, cluppenguln, beyoncebeytwice, nerdsigh, 5thdivinebeast, jenniferlarencesnapped, read-eat-sleep, ghostcop, clitpotle, ughsammy, youphoric, aha-itsme, beyoncevevo, notchicken, adolescent-lycanthropy, synapolitan, trust, aquajoggers, nintenclo, itsnot-anselelgort, whatsacanada, detectivejakeperalta, melniikova, the7thtrigger, sassycappy, youeitherskateoryoudie, benedictcumberbath

"The New England Vampire Panic"
>ronweasley, ninetails, equalistmako, stachionalgeographic, imanes, twyrinehaze, smallnico, marzipanandminutiae, titleleaf, lgb-positivi-t,

respectfulmemes, jaredduck, avoidantcactus,
positive-lesbian-vibes, bitchybreadpainter,
littlebirdofprey, catvampire, majestic-space-
dragon, thecaffeinebookwarrior, chuanfakitty,
just-shower-thoughts

"seventeen thousand dollars"
twisteddoggeh, amberfanblog, marauders,
friendlyneighbourhoodpizzaman, bigspender, palavra-
valise, spinningyarns, chibibuizel, pixelscalemate,
nick-nellson, natasalways, puppytierjade,
itabia, robotsatthedisco, seifukucat, asphyyyy,
dingdongyouarewrong, not-burnie, dognova,
weavemunchers, baracknobama, dashconstaff,
icrnpatriot, twilve, greglestrade, babygirlvinnypizza,
jokesmymomwouldlike, protagonistheavy, gaymzee,
butch-king-frankenstein

"Super and Who and Lock"
sherli-holmes, littlenim, purple-shirt-of-sex,
cumbersome11, thetimelordwizard, zpaze, welcome–to-
the-madhouse, sourwolf-loki-destiel-221b, gothicprep,
sherlockpining, mymindpalaceisatardis, chloomydiaa,
quinzel-isley, allforhisgreaterglory, tyrannny,
shouldertappingghosts, tyleroakley, burgrs, royhvrper,
robotmango, charlie-the-badger, teacupsandcyanide,
sixcatsandtwodogs, kyrart, apushinthewrongdirection,
911official, banrions, disasterlarper,angelicpooper, ducky-
tm, 11-faces-and-counting, higheldertala, the-fandoms-are-
cool, vivianandhersocalledlife, icantdotheonesteptwostep,
stacysdad, a-study-in-gay, keenling-superwholock-whore,
haiirflip, buckywasherebuckywasqueer

"girl autobiography"
memories, the-worm-man, glumshoe, equestrianpotato,
more-notes-than-you, flutejesus, wheelernancy,
blluish, officialaudreykitching, tenyonepilots,
andsjuliet, zackisontumblr, samingtonwilson,

greenmossloveisreal1998iloveyou, leisures,
parabins, marauuders, 6i, fuckstev, rue-
bennett, mainmanblackdynamite, weaver-z,
nowthatswhaticallblogging

"I Swear We Were Misha" and "Confessional"
potatofuzz, lunarsailor, gothicprep, cyberiamix, belleuse,
squirrelbro, ziggystarfishh, agentdaisymaximoff,
fineyoungsatanist, wearesorryfortheinconvenience,
piratescarfy, chloemoretsblog, lovethroughthedarkdays,
eleventhwhovian, raggedydoctorgoodnight,
cameronjohngodfrey, killercest, bowlegsandangels,
sooptheawesome, theredseraph, sublimesublemon,
watsonly, ohshititsgreg, guardianofthebeam,
watchtheskytonight, communitytv, elisabtch, i-could-
be-so-much-more, nick-nellson, madturbating, snaafu,
youthful-sinner, bilbutt-baggins, kikistiel, fun-with-
fandoms, deatofabachelor, mostlytins, felicityallxn, come-
along-p0nd, jackhawksmoor, sentirlanada, pantlesshero,
smallherosix, 2019metgala, the-doctor-of-the-bakerstreet

"A Creation Myth"
captaincrusher, aquariushawty, marisatomay,
cahootings, mypetufo, jew-gi-oh, dduane, iwatobigreg,
astudyintransience, morethanslightly, habitualshaker,
anglelica, amaltheas, partygoerpropaganda,
90stvqueen, lucifer-is-a-bag-of-dicks, sepulchritude,
foulserpent, foolsforthought, bademjanboy, meta-xylene,
snorlaxatives, xyle, bookslayer13, brunz, sagihairius,
perfectionistdia, whorusszahhak, shouttogether, c1efairy,
ferris-bu3ller, susiethemoderator

"missing e."
Regretfully, no source data exists for this poem.

"They Don't Say" and "Monster Girlfriend"
dirtydanvevo, gerudoe, coatfloat, dining-and-
pining, egberts, lenarise, catholicnun, turnmy,
pantheisticsunshine, promiscuous-petal, rattlegore,

mmmgrayons, bombing, psalmsnotbombs,
xbluemetgreen, fake-ketchup-blog, nooktoobomb,
nemohamoran, somethingpointy, rnerrychristmas,
wereyoulookingforsomething, officialwhitegirls, staraptor

"[CENSORED] energy"
wheel-of-fish, haiikyuus-remade, yors, paperlesscrown,
stardustschild, poupon, catherinemiddletons,
steamandsequins, dingdongyouarewrong, granny-
core, peachcookie, henstopper, killstomper,
lucytara, cringeassremakingnaenaebaby, swainlake,
hearthstoneblitz, warriormale, beachdeath, bramble-star,
magicalmystic, marzipanandminutiae, rainbowgaez,
phendranadrifts, foulserpent, oberynmartell,
tealesbian, dancefloors, luchadoreofliberty, cool-town,
hymnsofheresy, saint-just, loneozner, heauxmeauxbeaux,
littlewichita, moonyjohnlupin, theboynexthodor

"an on and off switch"
yourdadsghoulfriend, nihilisticqueen, revretch,
letmebegaytodd, yuyuuyuyuu, grxnite, lilcowgirl7,
chimpanzeedotcom, fawnlimbs, tennantbutt,
1moneychasinworld, 1617, brownbearbutch, intensional,
glyphsmash, harrison-ford, my-gender-is, hootersasuke,
wizardonline, kazrietvelld

"The Bone Discourse"
blackfairypresident, tikkunolamorgtfo, geltoothpaste,
chmartx, hellphine, not100bees, sonypraystation, kasnas,
pastel-prouvaire, tired-internet-addict, nopathfollowed,
stxrks, thecapslockbrony, puppycommander,
captainimprobable, unseenphil, cutlerish, twilve,
fuckinheathen, the-ruby-queen, peachdeluxe,
mistflowerwitchcraft, the-way-rain-falls, needlekind

"I THINK I LOVE THE COLORS OF THE SKY UNTIL"
mrpotterbydia, gusmen,
hallandoates1970topresent, internetexplorers,
bigffatfeminist, ironyofchokingonjacksdick,

golden-soulll, ihuggedmikeyday, madturbating, thelilnan, transfigurationsgonnacome, abigaillx, narc0tixx, tupacabra, fungi, amongstwoodedpaths, makee-mee-beautifuul, mianaya, myskinnylife-blog, nonbinary-nicolo, therealhamster, grubbsgrady, i-only-know-fandoms, mrs-karkalicious, hashtagloveloses, god---sammit, silverleavesredskies, strawberrydaydreams, snowwhitestitching, corgay-blog, timrigginz, shadowrawrs, 2treehill, nowaitwhat, jezuzgodoffriendship, winter-soldier, gynocologist, supernaturalzeppelin-blog, hugt0wer, sumonlou, twilve

"There will be no sociology in the apocalypse"
a-shadowhunters-horcrux-blog, stedes-bonnet, gothicprep, pippiphooray-blog, mrauders, chharliedayarchive, danglingthpider, ulibeanz, limitlessotp, copperbooms, fasterfood, pikeisaman, hateruess, volar-e, drdoofenshmirtz-remade, hashtagloveloses, opalbeifong, positivemilkhotel, iansbowlhaircut, buyyourstruly, francieum-blog, theyellowbrickroad, thisurlisunavailable, nopehaz, guyramsayfieri, squidmama, junitanotjuanita, bakura, thegoldernsnitch, danisnottouchingbutts

"Smoking sections"
ppppbbt, dragongirltitties, pajamasecrets, rottenbutrecovering, the-flapwagon-archives, happiersuggestion, wattpadfic, thatdiabolicalfeminist, fogblogger, cheerfullygoth, notlindsay, starting-to-feel-just-right, offensivebeach, marzipanandminutiae, wetsnail, freifraufischer, queen-of-the-merry-men, angelictrauma, lordoftheinternet

"A Growing List of Banned Tags"
nobodynocrime, twilve, sketiana, mjwalker-writing, jddryder, stuckinapril, galacticjerk, rawhoneybliss, scaryorganmusic, collarboen, dingdongyouarewrong, miiilowo, beachnet, iamalivenow, vigilantsycamore,

detasteful, savoiardi, teenagerposts, the-tryhard-twihard,
tenorgender, solongfranklloydwright, exeggcute,
stefito0o, bannedtags, ladiesblr, aluka, rue-bennett,
slippinkimmy

"Four Thirteen"
doktorivan, dooplissss, pinnedbutterfly, scriptures,
eridansmatesprit2, bhreac, penotbutter, fungasm2,
ahilaughingalonewithpepsi, cowprintbuckets,
deathbuster-blog, shadeshipster, pelvicthrustingahobo,
drunkenfixx, yourconfessions, forthehoundsofhell,
dualscar, meirz, drinkball, brolyssa,
homestuckheadspastedontothings, gonnaslapaboo,
nextlevelnomad, trainedbrofessional, hankhillsbooty,
rappinpicard, lizzledpink, geromy

"Booped"
krash-8, viewfinder-chernobyl, theghostofmusicman,
piedude, mestruazioni, tearlessrain,
thedogeveryonehates, a-canceled-stamp, toss-a-coin-to-
your-stan-account, smug-puppy, randomly-not-knowing,
lzrdprsn, peniswizard69, disgustinggf, cloverstellar,
catilinas, anachronic-cobra, transvampireboyfriend, oh-
munda-kukkad, kamaal-da, rickybabyboy, userparamore,
pierog, 3friesshortofahappymeal, kittengutss,
stuckinapril, miamignonette, fairyborderl8ine,
bizarrelittlemew, oxydate, pathologicalreid, drops-of-
universe, sotibllec

"still life of a romance"
weedjoke420, jurassicswamp, kawoooparade,
returnofthejudai, gurlskum-blog, benlovedogs, nyx-010,
theelliedoll, politicallyobsessedscholar, oldwizardboots,
thecommonchick, dirkdammit, theforce, heathens-and-
kings, alrightevans, gothicprep, hijacker, crplpnk, stuck-
stateside, vuls, arcticbubbles, danielkanhai

"My body becomes a riot"
brendanicus, 1989taylorsversion, just-shower-thoughts,

lloras, parksrway, pawcakes, lateafternoonsunlight,
yenvengerberg, benjamingross, tri4l-and-t3rror,
sapphicscience, 1dietcokeinacan, annabelleloren,
futuresabove, yamelcakes, groupieculture, prairiies,
noodleincident

"The Morally Grey Cinematic Universe"
jewishbarbies, puppetwithapistol, chaitealattyay,
swarnpert, gxnya, hyrude,wtiom, shrimpsisbugs,
persianflaw, spidaerman, rattlegore, rainbowgazes-
archive, silk101, okayysophia, longseasons,
abutterflyobsession, lovequinn, karalovesallthegirls,
thegoodvybe, lingrix, thexfiles, gnarlygnat,
twentyoneamigos, kristina100000, lamotteling,
atasteoflee, chunkecheeks

"Terms of Service"
twilve, goodmendontneedrules, mysterioushceekbones-
and-bowties, hashtagloveloses, ihopebarackobama,
whiskyandtea, deathbysharpie, yorkshirepudding,
doctorwho, santa, secytardis-, scarjoboobshasmoved,
perny, rocksoncubatron, bergmanns, nick-
nellson, whistleandaclick, danieljradcliffe,
queenofsevenkingdoms, ginandweas, melaudrama,
cybermans-blog, never-apply-logic-to-who,
benedictcumberbatchseyebrows, bicorn, armlarnators,
enemy-of-the-capitol, crazyyetsane, doctor-who-
companion, ohmymyeolchi

"This is how it started, back then" and "Gay Histories"
dingdongyouarewrong, curbstompmeplz, voyria,
hustlerose, thebridgesandtunnels, niurefine, bogleech,
theconcealedweapon, absurdly-useful, enoughtohold,
inspirationawe, thecoggs, mlarayoukai, drcuriousvii,
cerastes, hxrnyonmain, dustsculptures, fertbutt,
naturallyevill, disease-danger-darkness-silence

"Okay."
marzipanandminutiae, marauders4evr, officialek,

the-other-ryan, mexicanheaux, zldg, crispy-ghee,
butch-king-frankenstein, merlinsbearditsthedoctor,
ink-phoenix, sixtape, lethelightshineonme,
v1als, artistformerlyknownasbutttrumpet,
jodiefoster, okheshivar, mrsskinnypenis, taemsgirl,
basedgodwasright, bonegrenade, pharahlesbian

"No Courts at Pride"
thatdiabolicalfeminist, ph4u57, bugghost,
supermegafoxyawesomehogwarts, coltre, hbunot,
girlwithapomegranate, aviolafyre, fresh-princess-of-
gallifrey, comradekits24, hempkitty, uncannyvalleygirl,
bruhleesi, drugmember, mgs1otacon, bodysanctuary,
tanoshindekouze, karkat-kanaya-mix, saladude, bidoof,
kinglesters, geltoothpaste, k5ataskia0z8o, bippycorgan,
hockey-princess, noxiousb, anthonyamorim, aconissa,
94li, vultureworth, jakeperalta, jumex, nomono-
perspective, tyleroakley, drmazel, precise-millipede,
thisclockworkheart, constantneverland, effington,
vygandonut, thelunarboy, lowerclass-uppercase,
just-shower-thoughts

"The Military Skeletal Industrial Complex"
forfuckssakejim, solsikkepop, conspiicuouss,
surprisebitch, lycanthropelesbian, vuls, mvtk42,
braginskey, ghostpulse, catgirlmadi, slihgtlydyslexic,
skeletonmeme, skelezor, lunalookalike, memguy-com,
infamousnfamous, ironychan, captainshroom, mx-
bones, thatonefrostycanadian, purgeparty, marxistically,
420meme-it, mythosblogs

"4chumblr"
jiyeong, chaoticbutterfly, soulofthedrill, matryoshika,
missmika, boyvandals, mikarella, monobeargrylls,
fuckyeah4chumblr, asdfasf20348951903845018925,
tumblrandanon, halfcharacter, 1lac, anonymousnoko-
blog-blog, fuckyeahrarepepes, iamalmostspartacus,
totallywicked, hwippedcream, tres-leches-blog,

derpingroberto, snakelinksonic, yoonas, reverse-trap,
thecommander, dylanbarrett, alittleriddle, chigen-
atomic, leahsoldblog, shutupmokuba, clickmesoftly-blog,
californiumoxide-blog, pottylurvesloony, sladez

"Fake Story Mad Lib" and "Tumblr Account as Doomed
Narrative"
reallyreallyreallytrying, lymphonodge, mosshound,
kim-jong-chill, mattheuphonium, tockthewatchdog,
officialstarscream, thewolfofnibu, haedia, geekishchic,
skymachine, djkoenig, continueplease, toplil,
theanimejunkie, thunder-blitz, slimetony, meladoodle,
soldmysoul4wifi, thegirlygeekinitiative, caitlincst,
egg-rolls, vodcar, leatherwingsinc, turkey-imported-
from-maine, lolsofunny, find-the-beauty-within,
gudram, laurelhach, cryptidfuckery, voyagevisuelle,
andhumanslovedstories, zaynmalikeatsass,
firelorcl, dailynarnia, oddbagel, annabellioncourt,
kinesthetiachomoromanticore, racheldaddow,
druggeddraccus, ttogamii, wizardnuke, tonystark-tm,
wingdingle, aru, paradoxsocks, dingdongyouarewrong,
darkmemeasstronaut, pizzaforpresident,
gallifreyanprincess, merlinsbearditsthedoctor, vodni,
abbysrwk, randomthingieshere, yourlocalpsychopath,
cloudyobsession, starkinglyhandsome, uberfaenatic,
prettyboyshyflizzy, dangerbooze, myfriendscallmemaury,
dad-monster, grymmoires, aurevoir-mes-amis,
mellowminty, wasereborworthit, moniker-padacklyte,
madamepompador, iwantfitbody, bunnyinafez, suklaaaa,
hypno-agnex, pebbles5ever, crossroadsbishounen,
karrius, watchthelightfade, gayfarmer, partywok,
purepopfornowpeople, unclefather, kikithegirl,
ironychan, ryanvoid

"Castiel's Girls"
nick-nellson, firstrising, pruningthisbranch,
officialokcupid, dgsafdmd, fshteeth, americachavez,

100493503004422, fineyoungsatanist, rneerkat,
lightly, clown-dick, trash1994, tennants-hair,
absolutemonarchist, caricalaic, lumos5000, distraughtiel,
murphels, eyelikeamagpie, e-liotss, 2pissymagpies,
confettistan, thisismydivision, thesherlockedboffin,
magifran-blog, raspharys, soundsrussiantome, zachabee,
rnushu, timey-wimey-avenger, handpiouslyfolded,
dontgigglesherlock, thetimelordwithnoname

"I Watch a Man Die on Television"
f-hudsons, finchel-feelings, twilve, autoneurotic,
i-could-be-so-much-more, avengered, randomsplashes,
fightforyourrighttosharpie, emilylupin, danieljradcliffe,
souaesthetic, darklords-and-daleks, steven-moffat,
susiephone, this--too--shall--pass, 69shadesofgray,
cptfunk, bakerstreetbabes, idonotlikethatsam-iam,
previously-gillany-blog, -robwoah, 4cidrain

"Continues To Lose Her Entire Mind"
dingdongyouarewrong, twilve, wlfgrlplus, melodoka,
marzipanandminutiae, lakevideo, dedicatedfollower467,
kingstooth, bakwaaas, frostedpuffs, grandfloridians,
sapphling, poutine-supreme, agonisingpain,
basedprincessdisorder, charlottan, musicalhell,
jennaortegas, nicework-bonedaddy, followthebluebell,
darkcomedies

"it comes in twos" and "Snoem (Snail Poem)"
rhubabe, badconlangideas, lesserjoke, snowqueenrue,
enchantedribbons, re-bee-key, woprqjfpasih, marypsue,
gnny, andrew-scotttt, fatherofthebride, foliejpeg,
floambones, robotmango, featherofficial, noshirtnoblouse,
drugsbust, xbox420, kuxco, rutaskadi, syndeux, meeplol,
egberts, witchjock, abomasnow, emilianadarling, clamjob,
nxte, lntelligent, gardenianoire, amporas, cvxdghrgdfnte,
ectoviolet, perfunctory

"I've never watched an episode of supernatural"
lesibansofboromir, martymcfly, flyingfalconflower12,

necronatural, lyeekha, zimtchai, mylittleredgirl, farmside,
parakeet, theheroichydrangea, magicalgirlmindcrank,
goblinpat, gaydestiny, beerecordings, tillman,
stimman4000, heritageposts, quinnfebrey, bastart13,
the-goblin-cat, witchervesemir, kaijuno, trevenanl,
elleroodles, dingdongyouarewrong, randomslasher,
kelvintimeline, normalgirl, devsbian, antifarichietozier,
podcastwizard, yourknightinshiningplastic,
elphabaforpresidentofgallifrey, romanroyalty,
americachavez, annevbonny, harrierdoobie

"The Cock Monologue"
fishingboatproceeds, ehjovan

"Pretty Girls"
captainlordauditor, farmtortie, jakeperalta,
ofdirtandbones, rodrickheffeley, pollyjean, slimegargoyle,
chaoticbisexualalien, deep-dish-luigi, jestersuccubus666,
thestateonmtv, gotginger, meladoodle, deadpresidents,
writtenskyes, debrides, jaxxgarcia, boobyguy,
priestessamy, bella-likes-nutella-and-acapella, alectually,
emiliusthegreat, flickerman, amythical-llama,
batmanisagatewaydrug, bassflutes, wheeloffortune-
design, emailmore, 6slut, damaramegido, blackkatmagic,
things-are-looking-up-oh-finally, soupdrag0n,
robertmitchum

"Goncharov (1973) dir. Martin Scorsese"
prettyboysdontlookatexplosions, zoewashburne,
almostsweetangel, xpoolboy, greenmp3,
overelegantstranger, lemonadeandlanguages,
busexualshakespeare, duckyyixing, tsscat, susiephone,
blackboxwarrior, saint-batrick, iphyslitterator,
hussyknee, penny-anna, bismuth-209, ragdoll-ren,
inoffizielles-deutschland

"THIS IS THE PLACE"
raspbeary-blog1, myhead-itskillingme, nachofather,
gatzzby, ohshit-demons, twilve, deancasotp,

henryandhisbrain, discolor3d, dankickedphilsstickz,
anniecrestaodairs, princessoftypos-blog, tauriel-of-
moondor, grabyougearhobbitsandhunters, heathlegder,
ambieheartsturtlep0rn, nyehs, 0ptimuspenguin, worb,
bubonickitten, emotionalfossil, undesired-pageblood,
fall-out-boy, avoiding-the-parentals, i-could-be-so-
much-more, petitfrenchie, cyberho, halfmundane,
pizza, nick-nellson, daffydthomas, shutupmerlin,
hashtagloveloses, hunterandrewpence, poecurl,
holnnes, rnemes, selfdoubtandsyphilis, twilve, coffee-
in-europe, pretensious, homofauxbic, choythirsty,
shonensumpreme, yung-queers, foreveralone-lyguy,
somberfawn, mmilhouse, elsenliberator, yugoslavic,
dingdongyouarewrong, timmynookremade-blog,
911official, simplymykayla

"Redemption"
dashcon-two, ladygolgotha, brilliantpines, somefangs,
serethereal, strange-aeons, cemeterygrace,
deancrowleycas, destiel-news-channel, lastoneout,
vexwerewolf, bigothteddies, homunculus-argument,
woman-becomer, ankle-beez, furryprovocateur,
campirejournalist, bearie, countess-of-edessa, the-
muppet-joker, cityyliights

"Youth"
zombiestorm-blog, padfootmagic, danieljradcliffe,
snivellys-trousers, fiftyshadesen, whtvr, yourconfessions,
concretedesign, itsallaboutstelena, kyui13, magical-
mischief, fatalattracti0n, nick-nellson, adisneytales,
thecolorblockcurator, thvnhv, ballzd33p, kanyeplsnot-
blog, istillhaveyou-, harrypotterconfessions,
veronicamarsconfessions, j00niedimples,
marzipanandminutiae, robertsheehanisgod,
ohyeahronhermione, cindalyv

Title Index

4chumblr	58
A Creation Myth	24
A Growing List of Banned Tags	37
an on and off switch	31
Booped	40
Castiel's Girls	60
[CENSORED] energy	29
Confessional	55
Continues to Lose Her Entire Mind	62
Four Thirteen	39
Gay Histories	50
girl autobiography	21
Goncharov (1973)	71
I love you in the new year	15
I Swear We Were Misha	23
it comes in twos	64
I THINK I LOVE THE COLORS OF THE SKY UNTIL	34

I've never watched an episode of Supernatural 65
I Watch a Man Die on Television 61
missing e. 26
Monster Girlfriend 73
My body becomes a riot 43
No Courts at Pride 52
Okay 48
Pretty Girls 69
Redemption 76
seventeen thousand dollars 18
smoking sections 36
Snoem (Snail Poem) 70
still life of a romance 42
Super and Who and Lock 20
Terms of Service 46
The Bone Discourse 32
The Cock Monologue 67
The Military Skeletal Industrial Complex 56
The Morally Grey Cinematic Universe 45
The New England Vampire Panic 16
There will be no sociology in the apocalypse 35
They Don't Say 28
This is how it started, back then 47
THIS IS THE PLACE 74
Tumblr Account as Doomed Narrative 78
Youth 80

First Line Index

A
A beautiful moment 80
a cat paw 40
at 2 in the morning 64

C
come forward 16
concept: woman making dear life 24

D
dear yahoo 74
December took with it like sex searches 37
Do you have a skeleton? 56

E
every girl i see is pretty 69

F
For $17,000 USD 18

G

Get your bottles ready 65
girl i'm sorry i think 43
Goncharov is a dream 71

H

he talks to me about 21

I

I CONFESS to Jane, a lesbian 34
I dream of a black dog, a Grim 32
Is it too late to be a deep 76
i stood next to him 50
it's a vulgar rain and the water asking 58
It's in our history 48
I was a first born child 'til I gave 20
I was a wild horse in your camera 78
i was out of smokes 36
i will be a timeless astronaut 73
I wish I loved him in the 19th century 45

M

My candy mouth, drained 67
My gender is a 31

O

OH MY GOD the   thing happened today 59
on tumblr they don't say "i love you" they say 28

S

sometimes, in secret 15
spiritual wellness culture 62

T

talent is overrated but when you said 42
the gay angel breaks 60
The Mishapocalypse comes to you like 23
The rules of the game change 46

This is how it happens 35
today is monumental 52
Tumblr: a whole new species. Watch 26

W

We all saw the picture: victim on a hot 61
we burst into giggles 47
when i was little i 55
When universes are destroyed 39

Y

You cannot sleep now 70
"your nipples are now 29

www.ingramcontent.com/pod-product-compliance
Lightning Source LLC
Chambersburg PA
CBHW010046090426
42735CB00020B/3404